Veiled Joy

A Memoir of 3 Years, 2 Gains, and 1 Loss

CATHY BROWN HATHAWAY

I have tried to recreate events, locales, and conversations from my memories of them. Some names and identifying details have been changed to protect the privacy of individuals. I may have changed some identifying characteristics and details such as physical properties, occupations and places of residence.

For information contact: cathat44@gmail.com

Book and Cover design by Laura Brown

ISBN: 978-1-941749-58-6
Library of Congress Control Number: 2016912355

4-P Publishing
Chattanooga, TN

First Edition: September 2016

DEDICATION

This book is dedicated to my siblings:
Vetta, Brucie, Bobran, William,
Mary Ann, Jen and Connie

CONTENTS

1

Prologue

The excited voices outside my room woke me early. I rolled over in bed with one eye open and noticed it was 9:00 o'clock in the morning. Stumbling to the door, I opened it and peeked out.

Girls were rushing back and forth. Relatives were looking for students. I jumped to attention as I remembered my 10:00 o'clock appointment at Sanford Stadium.

While rushing to the shower, I reminisced about my parents. They walked this same hall after leaving me on my own for the first time. I called it freedom. They called it college. That was three years ago.

The day Mom and Dad dropped me off at college was the best day of my life. But, it was also the beginning of an underlying tragedy that has taught me lessons that college could not.

We don't always realize we're in the midst of the storm until it passes. The clouds move on. The sun comes out. You can see clearly again.

After marching into Sanford Stadium with my black gown and yellow tassel blowing in the wind behind me, I did see clearly again. With my degree tucked under my arm, I waved at everyone and reflected on the pass three years. I understood that life is not obligated to me. I have to take the good with the bad. The best years of my life were also the worst.

"The aim of education is the knowledge, not of facts, but of values."

William S. Burroughs

2

Joy

I remember standing in the doorway of the bedroom I shared with my sisters. The blue chenille spread covering the bed was filled with clothes and all the essentials needed for college. The bunk beds held luggage, a radio, hot plate, iron, clock and all the things Mom discarded for lack of packing space.

While absently listening to Mom chatter about my new adventure, I glanced at the painting on the crème colored wall and remembered the fun my siblings shared painting the scene of a deer standing by a lake. We painted by numbers, and we painted when we had a notion. It may have taken a few days or a week, but eventually, the scene was finished. That painting was a treasure.

I focused my attention on Mom again and wondered how she could pack so many clothes in one piece of luggage. She reminded me to keep a sewing kit on hand. Standing 5' 0", every dress I owned had to be hemmed. She also repeated her instructions on hair care. She knew my black, shoulder length hair was not a priority for me. As she packed my make-up, I shouted "I need that." Her response was, "You don't need to paint your face."

"It's an enhancement, Mom."

"It makes your light complexion look like a dough face." That was an encouraging remark! She gave me that endearing smile as she closed my luggage.

Was I ready for college? No question. College was always a given - the proper progression of things. Mom and Dad did not have to speak the words and I didn't have to be coaxed. I wanted to see beyond the city limits of my hometown. I wanted freedom.

My parents were jewels. They were strong Christians and Dad was a very strict, no-nonsense disciplinarian. I've always had a healthy fear of him. His voice usually had a serious tone and to disobey him meant consequences. My brother was a mischievous teenager. Once, when he and several friends got in trouble, he came home and started reading the Bible. He knew the only person that could save him was God.

I was really in awe of my Dad. I thought he was superman and could leap tall buildings in a single bound. He was tall, dark and muscular. "My dad can do anything," I thought.

Sometimes, I still picture myself as a little girl

holding Daddy's big, strong hand. He was my security, my rock. When we asked Mom if we could go places, she said, "Ask your Dad." When we asked Mom for money, she said, "Ask your Dad." When we asked to join extra-curricular activities at school, ... "Ask your Dad."

I recall Dad's commitment to taking us to college at the appointed times after summer and semester breaks. Many times he would work 10 hours, come home, shower and change clothes, get back in the car and drive us to Athens, Georgia which was 3½ hours away. After dropping us off at school, he would get back in the car and drive home. Superman!

College was an adventure. New place. New people. New experiences. I felt like the country girl Ellie Mae Clampett arriving on the campus of the University of Georgia. Ellie Mae hadn't been exposed to a lot outside of home, but she was ready for anything.

"Gee Pa. Look at the tall buildings. Look at all the people from other countries. There's a big ole bus. The students are gittin' on the bus. Where you reck'n they going, Pa?"

"Well, Ellie Mae, I reck'n that big ole bus is

takin 'em to class. I red up on the school. I recollect they's 10,000 (35 years ago) students here."

"10,000 students?! I ain't neva seen that many people in one place, Pa! I cain't wait for Granny ta see it!"

I was amazed and slightly overwhelmed at the campus, the buildings, and the people. But, having two sisters already there made for a smooth transition. I wasn't a stranger; I was with my sisters. When I didn't see them, I knew they were there.

Creswell Hall was my home away from home for 3 years. It was a freshman dorm, but it felt so familiar and comfortable, I decided to return each year. Its green panels reminded many students of a green monster, hence the name 'Big Green Monster'. Some called it 'The Well' or 'C-Well'. I called it 'Creswell'.

There were lounges on each floor and a spacious lobby for studying, relaxing and entertaining guests. A large sign in the lobby displays the dorm motto: Live Well, Learn Well, Creswell.

My first experience with streakers was at Creswell. I was leaving the dorm for class when a herd of naked male students from Georgia Tech ran through the lobby. I stopped dead in my tracks, wide-eyed, mouth open and thought, 'If Dad could see this, he would make me come home!' The retreating backside of naked men is an image I didn't soon forget.

I later learned that the University of Georgia and Georgia Tech were friendly rivals in the number of naked students streaking through campus! What an accomplishment! I'm not sure who holds the record today.

Sanford Stadium, usually associated with the Georgia bulldogs football team, was the site for graduation. Normally filled to capacity on football Saturdays, it is one of the most beautiful and electrifying arenas in the country. Often referred to as 'between the hedges', on graduation day, it was surreal. Black caps and gowns replaced red jerseys and football helmets. Proud parents and family members replaced enthusiastic fans. Tailgating alumni were replaced with excited friends sharing their dreams.

"Some people drink from the fountain of knowledge, others just gargle."

Robert Anthony

3

Clueless

H ave you known someone who was traveling somewhere, but not quite sure of their destination? That was me.

"What is your major?" I was asked.

"Uh-h-h..."

Journalism appealed to me. I pictured myself on television as a news commentator. That was my first year. Journalism didn't stick.

How about sociology? Sounded interesting.

Um-m-m...?

Didn't like sociology. That was my second year.

Political science sounded good. "That's it," I thought. But, my heart wasn't in it. And, because of that, I was an average student and did just enough to get by. I'm ashamed to tell my son my grade point average from college. He graduated college with honors.

I had a friend in college who was a genius. She never studied, but was an 'A' student. God gave her something he didn't give me. I pretended to possess this gift and not study. Bad idea!

I took a personality test for college majors on homeworktips.com. The results were interesting :

"You are a Conventional Personality Type!

Conventional people are fond of history and they like to observe holidays. They are traditional, and they like to know exactly what is expected of them in every situation. They are practical and very structured.

Conventional people might be good at math, but they may not want to work with numbers a lot. They can usually fit in to any group, but they don't necessarily want to lead all the time. They are not too interested in talking about feelings or deep relationships.

Possible degree programs were: Teaching, History, Nursing, Accounting, Computers, Finance, Real Estate, Insurance, Research, Business."

The personality description was on point, but none of the college degree programs interested me. That only proved one thing; I needed to figure it out myself. No one knows better than you what's in your heart.

It's true that a college major does not predict or guarantee your future. I read a few job statistics from the U.S. Department of Labor which show the average twenty-something switches jobs once every three years. The average person changes career fields two or three times in their lifetime. I strongly identify with these stats. In my search for the right fit, I changed jobs every three years and changed fields three times.

I was ready to take on the world when I graduated with a BA in political science.

The years that followed were disappointing because most jobs required experience. How do you get experience when everyone requires experience? Choose a major that's marketable! And then...keep putting one foot in front of the other.

My husband chose business and marketing as his major. He now runs a successful financial services business. My son decided, in junior high school, to be an engineer. He majored in engineering and today works in that field as a manager for Amazon. I'm a retired Postmaster and still don't know what I want to be when I grow up!

"All real education is the architecture of the soul."

William Bennett

4

Rules of the Road

Collage can be a tough transition when your parents have done everything for you. Learning to fend for yourself doesn't happen overnight.

My first roommate was a free spirit. She was 5 feet tall with long stringy blond hair and dressed like a hippie. We didn't try to be buddies, but we got along fine by staying out of each other's way. She was intelligent and studious.

Our room was spacious with a twin bed, desk, closet and chest on each side. There was an imaginary line down the middle which marked each domain. Your domain was the side you kept clean, but my roommate was not very tidy. She and I did not discuss the 'rules of the road' when we met.

But, I didn't think I needed to ask her not to leave her dirty underwear in the middle of the floor. Being a neat freak, that didn't set well with me. After we discussed her lack of consideration, her dirty underwear was no longer on the floor. It was left on her bed! Of course, that *was* her side of the room!

My second roommate was 5' 3" with shoulder length blond hair. She was personable and easygoing. We had similar backgrounds and related to each other well.

She invited me home with her to meet her parents and boyfriend. We had dinner together and enjoyed relaxing and focusing on something other than studying. It was a good weekend!

Shortly after that weekend, I was in bed one night and heard a male voice across the room. Again, we did not discuss the 'rules of the road'. But, I didn't think I needed to ask her not to allow her boyfriend to stay the night in our room. They were actually in bed.

I said, "Get him out of here!"

"We're not going to do anything!"

"You got that right! Get him out!"

I was assigned a roommate my 3rd year, but she didn't show up. Left with a private room, I relished the peace and quiet. I used the quiet time to map out my post-graduation plan:

The PLAN

    1) Move to Atlanta

    2) Secure a high salary job in criminal justice

    3) Marry a rich man

    4) Have 5 children

    5) Purchase a home with white picket fence

    6) Live happily ever after

Two out of six isn't bad!

"Follow your passion, stay true to yourself, never follow someone else's path unless you're in the woods and you're lost and you see a path then by all means you should follow that."

Ellen Degeneres

5

Fitness

I graduated high school at 132 lbs. Back then, that was fat. What I would do today to be there again.

The 'Freshman 15' usually comes after starting college. I brought it with me. And, late night studying and socializing led to late night eating. Consequently, no breakfast; the last thought after a late evening. My GPA could have used that energy boost from breakfast.

I decided to lose weight. My introduction to Weight Watchers was a sad awakening. I had no idea how to put together a balanced meal. I ate what Mom put in front of me. When it was time to prepare my own meals, I was lost. Weight Watchers was a good plan.

However, for me following the plan meant eating more than usual. I gained weight!

Bummer!

Not to be beaten, I decided to get fit. I couldn't afford to hire a trainer. I couldn't afford to join the gym. Why not take two fitness classes during the same semester and receive credits for elective courses?

I signed up for swimming and tennis. Swimming was a good choice. Knowing the life jacket

I wore while jumping into the deep end would save me didn't keep me from panicking. The panic passed. I kept jumping in and learned to swim to the side of the pool. My form wasn't the best, but I could stay alive.

Tennis was an excellent choice. I loved tennis. Before playing in local tennis leagues, I spent lunch hours at the park watching tennis matches. Playing tennis took me to another zone that was stress free. I've made many great friends on the tennis court.

Weight Watchers, swimming, and tennis - the beginning of my weight loss journey. I did lose the freshmen 15, but the battle of the bulge continues.

I also needed to get my finances in shape. With loans, grants and work-study, college is a major expense. But, I had my parents and no worries. I've always had a 'live in the moment' mindset. Focusing on today kept me from worrying about tomorrow. It took a decade to pay-off student loans, but college was worth every cent invested.

College taught me budgeting. My expenses were covered. I didn't need much, but I wanted a lot. The meal plan was included, but I chose to grocery shop, cook my meals and save money. I knew the bounty in the dorm vending machines – everything a college student could imagine.

Between my modest cooking skills (my hot plate served me well), vending machines, Krystal and the Shrimp Boat, I ate well.

Krystal was across the street from Brumby Hall, a five-minute walk from Creswell. It was a broke student's dream, 4 burgers for $1.00. So-o-o good! The downside was everyone knew what you had for lunch. The gas smelled exactly like the burgers. We called them 'fart' burgers.

The Shrimp Boat was next door to the Krystal. It was considered excellent cuisine for the non-discriminating palate; everything fried at a reasonable price. Thank goodness they accepted checks. We floated many-a-check in that boat.

"Be who you are and say what you feel,
because those who mind don't matter and
those who matter don't mind."

Dr. Seuss

6

Slipping Away

Mom was always lingering in the back of my mind. I usually thought of her working at home. With eight children, there was always work. Laundry was an everyday affair.

I remember her singing. She had a beautiful voice - a sweet sound to a child's ears.

She was fair skinned, 5' 6" inches tall, with beautiful long black hair. She often wore her hair in a French twist. My friends thought she was elegant.

I thought she was passive, but a better description would be a quiet spirit. It appeared that Dad ruled, but Mom was the glue that held us together.

Mom was a genius at stretching a meal, and it was always good. She made tea cakes for treats. Sundays were special. We ate twice as much for breakfast after Dad led devotion. He prayed (and prayed and prayed) and we all repeated the Lord's Prayer. If we learned nothing else from Dad, we learned the Lord's Prayer.

The smell of dinner at home after school was like anesthesia. "Ah-h-h. Home. Mom is here waiting to take care of me," I thought. Dinner was ready. Not in a few minutes, but when you walked through the door.

Sunday dinner was also special. Dinner after church was the best meal of the week. We might have had a huge roast with banana pudding made from scratch. Mom passed her excellent cooking skills to her children. I don't use mine.

I watched Mom make dresses without a pattern. "I can do that," I thought. I took a wide-tail black Mexican skirt, cut holes for the arms near the waist, folded the waistband inward for the neckline and wore it as a dress over a white blouse. A designer original!

My sister, Barbaree, was also creative. She had the bright idea to make a suit using burlap sacks. She made a skirt with a long matching vest which was very pretty. Dad didn't share our fondness for her designer original. He didn't want her to wear it.

One of the best memories of my mother was receiving a letter from her with $5.00 enclosed. Back then, $5.00 was a lot of money for a broke college student. I didn't ask for it. She had me on her mind.

During my early elementary school years, I remember walking with Mom to the Beauty Shop. I skipped, talked and played on the way. At the Beauty Shop, I watched the talkative stylist work magic with

Mom's hair. Pleased with the results, Mom smiled all the way home.

I also remember looking forward to Mom hosting her Women's Club. The fancy ladies would gather for their monthly 'me time'. They talked and ate delicious snacks. I would sneak to the end of the hallway and listen to the business discussed and juicy stories. Those stories were funny to a child, but outrageous to an adult.

One fancy lady asked if anyone had heard about the male teacher who obviously came to work without wearing underwear. He walked around all day with his hand covering his privates. During the day he had one class lined up outside the classroom longer than usual and had a pretty young lady in the classroom with him. The comments on that story ran the gamut.

After the Club meeting, my siblings and I had a party with the leftovers.

The summer I left for college, my mother started losing her hearing. At the time, I didn't know the extent of her health problems. I watched Dad take her to many, many doctors for evaluations. I felt guilty for my lack of patience as she descended into a world of silence. I didn't think about what she was dealing with. I only thought of myself.

There was no medical reason for Mom's hearing loss. I've learned that hearing loss is the 3rd most common health problem in America. One out of every 3 people between 65 and 74 years of age has experienced some level of hearing loss. Mom was only 42.

Years of exposure to loud noises may also damage the ears. Some work places expose the ears to dangerous noise levels, but Mom never worked in loud environments. Discounting 8 rambunctious children, she was not exposed to loud noises.

Doctors checked her ears for wax build-up, but her ears were clear. Her hearing loss was a mystery.

I've also learned that some medications may cause diminished hearing and problems with balance. I don't know the medications Mom took, but I did notice her balance was off when she walked.

I did not understand what was happening. Dad's answer to questions was, "She's sick."

Well... I knew that!

"Don't ever underestimate the importance you can have because history has shown us that courage can be contagious, and hope can take on a life of its own."

Michelle Obama

7

Saving Grace

My second year of college opened the door to life in a sorority. Some say fraternities and sororities cause division. Those are probably the ones who have not joined.

Pledging a sorority was probably the best thing, aside from getting a degree, that happened to me in college. I followed my two sisters who pledged on the charter line.

It wasn't about partying 'til you drop. It was about lifelong friendships, having a support system and getting involved in the community. On a university campus with a handful of African Americans, we looked forward to the comradery with other sororities and fraternities.

I met my college sweetheart, Lee Mackey, at a fraternity party. He was attracted to the mini dress I wore as I walked up the stairs in front of him. I was surprised he wasn't attracted to my girlfriend. Her dress was so short you could see her name and address.

The sorority gave me my first leadership

position, Dean of Pledgees. I took my responsibility for the pledgees seriously. I protected them. My name was Big Sister Tuf' Enuf'. I was tough on the surface, but dazed underneath – thinking of Mom. A tough exterior doesn't always mean a tough interior.

I've been told you should surround yourself with people you aspire to be like. My sorority was those people. It continues to draw wonderful friends and provides a network of amazing women. (Skee-wee!)

I thought of my sorority while reading this prayer by Mary McLeod Bethune:

"Father...We are glad to be called Thy children, and to dedicate our lives to the service that extends through willing hearts and hands to the betterment of all mankind...Grant us strength and courage and faith and humility sufficient for the tasks assigned to us."

"The world is more malleable
than you think and it's waiting
for you to hammer it into shape."

Bono

8

College Sweetheart

After meeting Lee Mackey, we talked on the phone for a short time and then began dating. I remember laughing when he said, "I've always wanted a red car and a red woman. Now I have both."

I sat many times in my dorm room window and watched that red car turn into Creswell Hall parking lot. I didn't wait for him to call upstairs. Downstairs I ran, anxious to see that electric smile.

Lee was tall, dark and good looking. He flashed a smile that was contagious. He was sweet but had a selfish streak. He looked good but didn't dress well. His attire didn't matter to me. I wanted a boyfriend and he was available.

Lee did not attend the university but had friends who did. He had an apartment in the city which gave me time away from campus. We spent a lot of time there. One momentous occasion was my one and only cat fight. He was seeing another girl while dating me. She was not only unattractive but also had my first name. She decided to come to his apartment, knowing I was there. She marched upstairs and retrieved some personal items from his bedroom.

Yes!

She did!

There was no time to think. I reacted with rage. I lunged at her with arms slinging.

Lee jumped between us, but not before I left my mark on her face. After he sent her away, I slapped him. Hard! His hand flew to his face, and he said, "That was a stinger!" I stared at him in disbelief. Breathing hard and wishing I had a weapon, I said, "Is that all you have to say?" He couldn't find his voice! I stormed out! He was history.

I was crushed. I threw myself a pity party which lasted several weeks. Then I decided to choose between pitiful and powerful. Powerful won. I shook him off and moved on.

After a few months, he began to call again. With no other prospects in sight, I opened the door to my heart again.

I saw unattractive namesake several times while riding the bus around campus. She would move from her seat on the bus to a seat close to me.

Really?

Mom told me not to play with crazy people. I took Mom's advice and ignored her.

One of my favorite quotes in college was from Longfellow:

"If we could read the secret history of our enemies, we should find in each person's life sorrow and suffering enough to disarm all hostility."

Unattractive namesake crushed that quote.

One beautiful, sunny day I was standing at a campus bus-stop, enjoying the weather and drinking a coke. I saw Lee drive by in namesake's car. I choked on the coke. Pounding my chest, I thought, "Did I just see what I think I saw?"

Instead of going to the dorm, I made a new plan. I hurried to a city bus stop and took the bus to his apartment. My legs were shaking as I approached his front door. There was no answer to my knock. I waited a few minutes as I listened to my knees knocking. That's when the light came on! Once! Twice! Not three times. I stood on his porch a couple of minutes to calm my knocking knees. I leaned against the wall and stared at nothing. Then I decided. This is the end!

After graduation, I moved to Atlanta. To my surprise, he showed up unexpectantly. He actually fell on his knees and begged me to take him back. I was shocked! Fortunately, he was out of my system. But, for a fleeting moment temptation's head rose because he looked better than he did before graduation. He had a new hair cut/style. His clothes were more fashionable than before and he had that same electric smile. But, it was over!

Having a strong spiritual foundation helped me get through that tough breakup.

That foundation was ingrained in me as a child. My parents kept us in church. Dad dressed in stylish suits with his classic shoes shined. Mom wore pretty dresses with her beautiful hair flowing. They proudly marched us to church *every* Sunday morning (*every* Sunday afternoon–BTU; *every* Thursday night–choir rehearsal).

Thursday night choir rehearsal took closeness to another level. Dad would pick up every child in the choir who did not live within walking distance of the church. We squeezed into our red and white Chevrolet station wagon and unloaded at Wesley Chapel A.M.E. Church. After an hour of half-hearted rehearsal, we squeezed back into the wagon and dropped each voice at their homes.

If we were too sick to attend church, we were too sick to go anywhere else. Staying in church kept us out of the streets. We were not just in church, we were busy. No one was a bench warmer. You had a role: choir, usher, pianist.

In college, I joined a campus ministry and made many new friends who shared my beliefs. My first college trip was a spiritual retreat to Gatlinburg, TN. Travelling to a ski resort was a first. Seeing that much snow was a first. Bonding with likeminded students was refreshing and motivating.

I was curious about other religions so I took a course in different religions around the world. It exposed me to other beliefs and broadened my perspective. My Christian beliefs were challenged, but not swayed.

"Don't just get involved. Fight for your seat at the table. Better yet, fight for a seat at the head of the table."

Barack Obama

9

Semester Breaks

I looked forward to going home for short visits after each semester because I didn't go home during the summer. I preferred summer school and working to sitting at home. There were not many social outlets or jobs for college students in my hometown.

During the short breaks, I saw Mom's health decline. I wasn't sure which came first, the hearing loss or the mental decline. I applaud Dad for continuously seeking help for her.

At the time, we didn't appreciate his efforts. Because she was getting worse, we thought he should do more. He did the best he could!

My younger sisters would relate frightening incidents of things that were out of character for Mom. One instance was when a neighbor called my Dad at work to tell him Mom was walking down the street naked. Of course, Dad immediately left work and went home. Another instance was my sisters coming home to find Mom with Dad's gun. She had not harmed herself or anyone else, but the possibilities were frightening.

I saw it. I heard it. I didn't understand it!

Mom reached the point of total silence. We

began communicating by writing notes. She became more withdrawn; physically present, but mentally absent. She became a different person.

I had looked forward to relating to her on an adult level. I also looked forward to our friendship. It never happened. I became angry. Who could I take the anger out on? Dad, of course - the one who was doing the most for her!

I've always been one for details. What's wrong? Why did it happen? When did it happen? When will it end? Can we take her to another doctor? Can we try a different medication?

Dad was not one for details. He said, "She's sick."

Okay!

He told me what he felt I should know. At the time, that was not enough.

I felt robbed. I was angry with Mom because in my young mind I thought she had left me. I didn't understand she had no control over her condition. I needed to talk to her about marriage, children, and homemaking. She had done all those things with grace. She was a phenomenal woman! Pretty. Hardworking. Committed.

Maya Angelou's poem, Phenomenal Woman,

reminds me of Mom. A few lines stand out to me...

Pretty women wonder where my secret lies.

It's the fire in my eyes,

And the joy in my feet.

The sun of my smile,

The grace of my style,

When you see me passing,

It ought to make you proud.

'Cause I'm a woman

Phenomenally.

Phenomenal woman,

That's me.

"It is impossible to live without failing at something, unless you live so cautiously, that you might as well not have lived at all; in which case, you've failed by default."

J. K. Rowling

10

A Lesson in Stereotyping

Working during college helped keep my mind off Mom. Those years were volatile times in our country. Racial segregation in schools was most prevalent in the South. Integration of schools was very new and had become a catalyst for civil rights action and racial violence.

At the time, African-Americans were not allowed to sit and eat in white owned restaurants nor enter to purchase food through the front door. My sister, Barbaree, and 2 friends decided to enter a restaurant through the front door. An angry patron used racial slurs and ordered them to leave. A fist fight started between the angry patron and one of my sister's friends. The owner of the restaurant separated them and told my sister and friends to leave.

After walking a few blocks from the restaurant, the angry patron drove past them and began shooting. I believe his intent was to scare them, because they were not injured. Someone in the neighborhood called the police and Barbaree and friends were safely escorted home. We were never told what became of the angry patron.

Another sign of the times occurred the first day of school after mandated integration. We were seated alphabetically in history class and I landed next to a white male. He instantly and angrily moved his desk away from me in a show of superiority. It didn't diminish my self-worth, but it was evidence of the cruel society we lived in. We are not born racists. We learn racism.

That same year I met with the school counselor to determine what classes I needed for high school graduation. Knowing I would go to college, I chose a few college prep courses. She said, "You won't need those." I took them anyway and refused to let her or anyone else hinder my path to success.

I worked as a research assistant to Dr. Stuart Surlin in the School of Journalism. Coming from a small town in South Georgia, I was accustomed to segregation. Black and white were all I knew. Seeing different nationalities existing harmoniously was something I had not experienced. Work-Study placing me in a job with a white man was not a surprise, but his liberal character was certainly different. Most white adults I had encountered were overtly prejudice. However, this man was different.

I never felt racial prejudice from Dr. Surlin. He always treated me with respect as his employee. He took me to lunch many, many times to the dismay of his fellow journalism professors. He escorted me around the offices where we worked like his star employee. The restaurant workers in the city were overtly prejudiced.

On one occasion, we drove to a restaurant in the city and parked directly in front of the entrance. The look on the restaurant worker's face was total disgust. You could cut his stare with a knife. Dr. Surlin ignored him, took me inside for lunch and made an unspoken statement to the restaurant worker and me, "You deserve to be here!" I was shocked and amazed by his character.

Dr. Surlin took me to his home to meet his wife and children. This was the first time I saw a child fly through the air. His two year old son decided to squat and poop on the floor. Dr. Surlin lifted him by one arm and swatted his bottom, sending him flying. Still held by his Dad, the toddler landed only to go flying again.

Dr. Surlin was the first white man who saw me as a person, and not as a black person. All white people are not racially prejudiced. That lesson has remained with me until this day. When I lean toward stereotyping, I remember Dr. Surlin.

"God wants us to know that life is a series of beginnings, not endings... Creation is an ongoing process, and when we create a perfect world where love and compassion are shared by all, suffering will cease."

Bernie Siegel

11

The Veil

T he doctors wheeled her away 2 hours ago. She should have returned long ago. Looking up to the sound of a hospital bed rolling through the doors, I saw the far-away look in her eyes. The shock treatments left her dazed. Her head turned slightly and without a word, she asked the question...

I turned the television off. The movie was depressing. It reminded me of Mom. My beautiful, strong mother had become more distant each time I went home. The doctor's visits, hospital stays, and medications were taking a toll on her. Most of her days and nights were spent in bed. She was angry with Dad. She believed he was trying to harm her. My siblings and I never believed or saw any evidence of this.

I've learned that believing things that are not true is a symptom of mental illness.

She no longer had the will or desire to cook and clean. If we asked, she would prepare special dishes. But, those delicious meals she once prepared were gone.

I've also learned that the inability to perform daily tasks is a symptom of mental illness.

Eventually, her friends stopped visiting. My grandmother became her only visitor. Most of their visit was in silence. Her presence was enough.

Mom's appearance began to change. She began to lose weight. Her facial features changed. She grew tired of communicating with notes and became more withdrawn. I yearned to talk with her. I remember, as a child, witnessing Mom talking to someone who wasn't there. I couldn't see them, but she apparently did. She had some heated conversations with this invisible person.

Hearing voices is a sign of mental illness.

I also remember Mom having a lot of headaches when we were children. I thought we were just getting on her nerves. Many times she sent me to Mr. Ed's Store to buy BC powders for her headaches.

Unexplained aches and pains are also a sign of mental illness.

Enough backtracking.

Shaking my head to clear the daze, I got up to turn the television back on. I punched the mute button and stared at the screen again. The woman in the picture's appearance had changed. She had lost weight. Her facial features were distorted. I thought,

"That's Mom." Images of Mom from the past three years ran through my mind.

There had been a cloud over my head for three years. I could finally identify the feeling of a veil over my face. I knew something was wrong, but I couldn't pinpoint it. I had been engrossed in college for three full years, having the best time of my life. But, that entire time, I had suppressed the feeling that I was losing Mom to mental illness.

Not wanting to think anymore, I punched the volume button on the television. The doctor was explaining mental illness to the patient's family. He said:

"Mental illness is a family affair. You need to talk about it. You need to learn about it. It is a disease. Fear and shame should not accompany it. Mental illness is real. You can't tell someone to cheer up or snap out of it. Recognize you can't fix it and seek professional help. You should treat the patient with respect, compassion, and empathy. Understand that you are not the victim, the patient is. You may go through denial, sadness, and anger. And then acceptance will come. You need to believe that no one is to blame."

I stood up and walked slowly to the large window in my room and stared at the tall trees dancing in the wind. "It all makes sense," I thought. Everything the doctor said applied to Mom. That was a hard pill to swallow. When sadness creeps in while thinking of Mom, I remember the doctor's words, "You need to believe that no one is to blame."

The underlying feeling of anxiety that haunted me in college has passed. At the time, I didn't recognize it. It didn't stop me. Quitting was not an option. But, getting through Mom's failing health showed me I could get through anything.

The veil had been lifted.

12

The Plan vs. Reality

Again, the PLAN:
1) Move to Atlanta
2) Secure a high salary job in criminal justice
3) Marry a rich man
4) Have 5 children
5) Purchase a home with white picket fence
6) Live happily ever after

The REALITY:
1) Move to Atlanta.

Moving to Atlanta was as exciting as the first day at the University of Georgia. The big city! I loved it and lived there 10 years.

    2) Secure a high salary job in criminal justice.

Every job I applied for in criminal justice was beyond my reach. I quickly learned to do what I could until I could do what I wanted. Encouraged to take typing in high school, I utilized that skill and took several secretarial positions while continuing my search for the high salary job in criminal justice.

Barbaree worked for the U.S. Postal Service and told me applications were being accepted. That was my turning point! I worked 11 years as a mark-up clerk forwarding the mail. I broke my record! For many years a mark-up clerk was not able to bid on other jobs. When that limitation was lifted, I bid on every job posted.

During those years as a mark-up clerk, I sought out temporary assignments and acquired experience in many areas. When the bidding limitation was lifted, I was prepared to spread my wings. Working in human resources, stations and branches throughout Chattanooga and the surrounding areas finally landed me the job of Postmaster. This was my dream job; no one looking over my shoulder, an office close to home, dependable employees and great customers.

3) Marry a rich man.

I've learned a good husband is better than a rich husband. Also, rich is relative. Some are rich in money while others are rich in love. I'll take a heaping helping of both.

4) Have 5 children.

After having one child, living in a new city with no known family and few close friends, I decided against having more children. My husband was not happy with my decision, but a difficult year with post-partum depression closed the door to more little ones.

My closest sibling was 2½ hours away. My close friends were scattered across the country. For my husband, adding a child to our family meant working harder and longer. I felt alone. New baby, new mom, and deep depression. I did not want to experience that again.

5) Purchase a home with white picket fence.

Barbaree encouraged me to buy my first home when I was 29. It was yellow with brown shutters and the perfect size for a single woman. It was a dollhouse without the white picket fence. I didn't realize I lived in a rough neighborhood until I heard rumors of home invasions.

I walked in on a burglary in progress. I had given a key to my boyfriend and told him he could take a television to his apartment. The television was on the floor in the vestibule, so I thought he was inside. Passing the vestibule, I noticed the lights were out, and the beams from a flashlight were glowing in the dark. The smell of cheap cologne and panic hit simultaneously.

I ran across the street and asked a neighbor to call the police. I saw a teenager run from my house and disappear in the dark. He took my best jewelry, but in his haste to leave left the television. He was never caught. My dollhouse was violated.

    6)   Live happily ever after…On target!

13

Inspirational Scriptures for College Students

Cathy Brown Hathaway

Good News Bible – Today's English Version

Jeremiah 29:11

"I alone know the plans I have for you, plans to bring you prosperity and not disaster, plans to bring about the future you hope for."

1 Timothy 4:12

"Do not let anyone look down on you because you are young, but be an example for the believers in your speech, your conduct, your love, faith, and purity."

Psalm 119: 9

"How can a young man keep his life pure? By obeying your commands."

Isaiah 40:29-31

"He strengthens those who are weak and tired. Even those who are young grow weak; young men can fall exhausted. But those who trust in the Lord for help will find their strength renewed. They will rise on wings like eagles; they will run and not get weary; they will walk and not grow weak."

Proverbs 23:19-21

"Listen, my son, be wise and give serious thought to the way you live. Don't associate with people who drink too much wine or stuff themselves with food. Drunkards and gluttons will be reduced to poverty. If all you do is eat and sleep, you will soon be wearing rags."

Psalm 71:5

"Sovereign Lord, I put my hope in you; I have trusted in you since I was young."

Ephesians 6:1-3

"Children, it is your Christian duty to obey your parents, for this is the right thing to do. Respect your father and mother is the first commandment that has a promise added: so that all may go well with you, and you may live a long time in the land."

1 Timothy 5:1-2

"Do not rebuke an older man, but appeal to him as if he were your father. Treat the younger men as your brothers, the older women as mothers and the younger women as sisters, with all purity."

Matthew 26:41

"Keep watch and pray that you will not fall into temptation. The spirit is willing, but the flesh is weak."

1 Corinthians 10:13

"Every test that you have experienced is the kind that normally comes to people. But God keeps his promise, and he will not allow you to be tested beyond your power to remain firm; at the time you are put to the test, he will give you the strength to endure it, and so provide you with a way out."

2 Kings 22:1-2

"Josiah was eight years old when he became king of Judah, and he ruled in Jerusalem for thirty-one years. His mother was Jedidah, the daughter of Adaiah from the town of Bozkath. Josiah did what was pleasing to the Lord; he followed the example of his ancestor King David, strictly obeying all the laws of God."

Micah 6:8

"No, the Lord has told us what is good. What he requires of us is this: to do what is just, to show constant love, and to live in humble fellowship with God.

Psalm 119:105

"Your word is a lamp to guide me and a light for my path."

Joshua 1:9

"Remember that I have commanded you to be determined and confident! Do not be afraid or discouraged, for I, the Lord your God, am with you wherever you go."

Philippians 4:8

"...fill your minds with those things that are good and that deserve praise: things that are true, noble, right, pure, lovely, and honorable."

1 Peter 5:7

"Leave all your worries with him, because he cares for you."

Proverbs 16:3

"Ask the Lord to bless your plans, and you will be successful in carrying them out."

John 14:27

"Peace is what I leave with you; it is my own peace that I give you. I do not give it as the world does. Do not be worried and upset; do not be afraid."

Psalm 105:4

"Go to the Lord for help, and worship him continually."

Colossians 4:5-6

"Be wise in the way you act toward those who are not believers, making good use of every opportunity you have. Your speech should always be pleasant and interesting, and you should know how to give the right answer to everyone."

Psalm 46:10

"Be still, and know that I am God…"

Matthew 7:7-8

"Ask, and you will receive; seek, and you will find; knock, and the door will be opened to you. For everyone who asks will receive, and anyone who seeks will find, and the door will be opened to him who knocks."

Philippians 4:19

"...my God will supply all your needs."

Isaiah 41:10

"Do not be afraid – I am with you! I am your God – let nothing terrify you! I will make you strong and help you; I will protect you and save you."

Acknowledgments

Thank you to:

My husband, Gary, for boosting my wavering confidence.

Coach Laura Brown, my awesome coach, for being the best instructor in the world.

Wayne Brown, my cousin, for watering the seeds.

Velma Wilson, my mentor, for your listening ear and candid straight talk.

My support team: Dollie Hamilton, Patricia Pace and Wenda Johnson.

My S.W.A.T. book camp friends: Angela Tanner, David Harrison, Donna Green, Jacquelyn Benford, Lisa Crawford, Micah Byrd, Pat Robinson, Sharonda Stiggers, Sylvia Banks and Zachary Tate

About the Author

Cathy Brown Hathaway is a retired Postmaster. She is active in church and community service organizations as a teacher, speaker, and musician. She is the founder of the Jewels of God (JOG) Ministry which provides mentoring for young adult women. She is also the founder of the Lovely Bones Book Club in Chattanooga, TN.

Veiled Joy is her second novel. She is also the author of *What Shall I Fear*, an inspiring novel of faith in the face of fear.

She resides in Chattanooga, TN with her husband, Gary. They have one son, Anthony.

Available for seminars, workshops, and motivational speaking. Call (423) 987-7321.

www.ingramcontent.com/pod-product-compliance
Lightning Source LLC
Chambersburg PA
CBHW071908020426
42331CB00010B/2716